BLACK DOG MUSIC LIBRARY

Beethoven: The Symphonies

BLACK DOG MUSIC LIBRARY

Beethoven: The Symphonies

Symphony No. 5 in C minor, *Opus 67*

Symphony No. 6 in F, *Opus 68, ("Pastoral")*

TEXT BY DAVID FOIL

BLACK DOG & LEVENTHAL PUBLISHERS
NEW YORK

Published by
Black Dog & Leventhal Publishers Inc.
151 West 19th Street
New York, NY 10011

Distributed by
Workman Publishing Company
708 Broadway
New York, NY 10003

Designed by Martin Lubin and Allison Russo

Special thanks Judith Dupré

Book manufactured in Hong Kong

ISBN: 1-884822-37-1

FOREWORD

*T*he symphonic music of Ludwig van Beethoven towers among the most remarkable artistic acheivements of all time. The structure and the genius, the grandeur and the beauty, the nobility and the passion, of Beethoven's Fifth and Sixth Symphonies challenge and stimulate the listener's mind and soul the first time one hears them, and the fiftieth.

Here in this volume you will be able to read and learn about Beethoven, the man and the composer; you will better understand the importance, the meaning, the message, and the structure of his great symphonic works; and you can enjoy and listen to the music as you read.

Play the compact disc included on the inside front cover of this book and follow along with the musical commentary and analysis. Please note that the times of the relevant musical passages are noted for your convenience.

Enjoy this book and enjoy the music.

Ludwig van Beethoven

On the frigid evening of December 22, 1808, an audience assembled in the Theater an der Wien in Vienna for what was to be one of the greatest and most challenging evenings in the history of music. The concert—or *Akademie*, as it was called—was a precious opportunity for Ludwig van Beethoven to premiere some of his new works. That historic program featured the world premieres of two symphonies, No. 5 in C Minor and No. 6 in F Major (their order and numbering were reversed on the program); two movements of the incomplete Mass in C; and the Choral Fantasy for piano, orchestra, and chorus (the latter composed at the last minute because Beethoven wanted his money's worth from the chorus he had hired). As if that program were not sufficient, he added his most recent piano concerto, No. 4 in G, and *"Ah! perfido,"* a twelve-year-old concert aria for soprano and orchestra.

"There we sat from six-thirty until ten-thirty in the most bitter cold," a member of the audience, Johann Reichardt, recalled, "and we found from experience that one could have too much even of a good thing, still more of a loud one."

Imagine this performance. None of the music had been sufficiently rehearsed, and the demands Beethoven's writing made on an orchestra of 1808, even one in Vienna, were staggering; there are suggestions that by the

Portrait of Ludwig van Beethoven by Josef Stieler.

night of December 22 the overwhelmed musicians were ready to mutiny. The ink was hardly dry on the orchestral parts for the Choral Fantasy—the concert's big finale—and there simply was no piano part. Beethoven, whose hearing at that point was little more than a memory, improvised at the keyboard while conducting the performance. Ultimately it collapsed in confusion over mistakes in the orchestral parts, and Beethoven had to get up from the keyboard and wade into the orchestra to correct the problem. The chaotic evening finally came to a close. Beethoven had just turned thirty-eight.

His Life

Ludwig van Beethoven (1770–1827) was a pitiful and miserable little man, beset with unending afflictions both psychological and physical. His childhood was the unhappy result of his parents' rocky marriage. Beethoven adored his paternal grandfather, also named Ludwig, who was a *Kapellmeister* (court music director). The old man thought his son Johann had married beneath him, and his bitterness further poisoned the already troubled young family. One son, Ludwig Maria, had already died in infancy when Ludwig van Beethoven was born on December 16, 1770, in Bonn. Issues of birth and relative aristocracy would always obsess Beethoven. He once went to court in Vienna to try to prove that the *van* in his name confirmed his nobility, and did little to stop the widespread rumor that he was the bastard son of Frederick the Great.

Johann van Beethoven seized on the emerging musical gifts of his oldest surviving son and enforced a teaching regimen that bordered on abuse. Johann saw Ludwig as a promising meal ticket, a boy genius he could exploit as successfully as Mozart's father had done his own son only a few years before. Johann did not possess Leopold Mozart's shrewd ear, however, and when Ludwig began to improvise and create—showing the kind of precocious talent that had filled the elder Mozart with joy—he became furious. The composer's childhood was a miserable one, so much so that as an adult he rarely spoke of it and professed to have forgotten the year and date of his birth.

By all accounts, Ludwig van Beethoven was a poor student, and the bulk of his musical training occurred outside his father's shadow. He was fortunate that his first composition teacher, Christian Gottlob Neefe, recognized his early promise as a composer. His first composition, a set of piano variations, was published when he was twelve. Still, performing was the only way at the time for a musician to make money, and Beethoven's

Beethoven's birthplace, Bonn

training included the violin, the French horn, and the piano. Among his first musical jobs was the post of assistant court organist in Bonn to the Archduke Maximilian Franz, who thought enough of the teenage virtuoso's ability to send him to Vienna in 1787, possibly to meet and study with Mozart. Whether or not these two giants actually met—and whether Mozart exclaimed over Beethoven's promise—is still argued. What is known is that

TROIS TRIOS
Pour le Piano_Forte
Violon, et Violoncelle
Composés et Dédiés
à Son Altesse Monseigneur le Prince
CHARLES de LICHNOWSKY
par
LOUIS van BEETHOVEN
Oeuvre 1.

Title page of Beethoven's Opus 1, *1795.*

Beethoven had to return to Bonn almost immediately, after learning that his long-suffering mother had died. At seventeen, he found himself responsible for providing for his two younger brothers, as his embittered father had started drinking heavily and could no longer support his family. Beethoven gave private lessons to make ends meet. His tutoring led to an important introduction to Count Ferdinand von Waldstein, who became his first great patron. It may have been Waldstein who arranged for Beethoven to meet Haydn when the renowned composer visited Bonn in 1790. Haydn is said to have encouraged Beethoven to come to Vienna to study with him and in 1792 Beethoven did so. The relationship did not last long, either because of personality conflicts or because of Haydn's travels. Beethoven then studied with Johann Georg Albrechtsberger and Antonio Salieri, whom he considered his real teachers, and began a series of productive relationships with noble patrons.

His brilliant debut in Vienna came in 1795, as soloist in one of his own piano concertos, probably the B-flat major concerto, now numbered his second. His fame as a musical phenomenon spread quickly, and he toured Europe as a soloist. Having Beethoven perform was considered a glamorous coup at Vienna's most aristocratic salons. Both his playing and his improvisatory skills left his fans in awe. He taught the most elegant figures in

Leopold Wing of the Hofburg. Beethoven performed in Vienna's most aristocratic salons.

Viennese society; one of his students was the Austrian Archduke Rudolf, to whom he dedicated the *Archduke Piano Trio*.

All of this changed as Beethoven approached 30 and became a victim of the cruelest irony that can afflict a musician—deafness. Why and how he was so afflicted continue to be a source of controversy. At the time, some claimed it was a manifestation of syphilis, while Beethoven himself worried that it was the result of his fearsome temper. The nature of his deafness suggests otosclerosis, a condition in which the auditory nerves shrivel and

the arteries around them become dilated. He suffered as well from tinnitus, a constant buzzing in his ears. Beethoven never gave up hoping for a cure for his deafness, which he pursued —without success—as vigorously as he did answers to his other medical problems.

At first he could not cope with his loss of hearing. His despair resulted in a frightening downward

Beethoven's hearing aid—an air trumpet—and the autograph manuscript of Eroica.

spiral that ended in the summer of 1802 in the Vienna suburb of Heiligenstadt, where he had gone to live. That fall he made the monumental decision to begin his life again, a choice he wrote about with heartrending determination in a manifesto known as the *Heiligenstadt Testament*. The testament was addressed to his brothers, to be read after his death, and it expressed Beethoven's anguish and rage at his growing deafness. He wrote about contemplating suicide and his reasons for choosing life. "It was only *my art* that held me back. Ah, it seemed to me impossible to leave the world until I had brought forth all that I felt was within me." Beethoven would be guided now by nothing but his need to express himself through music, and in this he became fanatical. "I live only in music," he wrote, "and I have scarcely begun one thing when I start another. . . . With whom need I fear to measure my strength?"

Beethoven's indomitable will yielded nothing to the world around him. In his remaining twenty-five years, he forged what was possibly the most dynamic period in the history of music: He pushed the boundaries of musical form and altered the very sound of music. He ignored the supposed limitations of performers and their instruments and furiously dismissed anyone who took exception to his work. When he read a nasty review of his *pièce d'occasion* titled *Wellington's Victory*—in fact, a piece of claptrap hardly worthy of him—he responded in a note to the critic, "You wretched scoundrel! What I shit [he used the German expletive *scheisse*] is better than anything you could ever dream up!" Beethoven's fierce personality, now unconstrained, drove even his friends away from him. He was paranoid, childishly jealous, and personally offensive. Though he insisted on solitude, he despaired of his loneliness, and failure greeted every one of his many attempts to find enduring love with a woman. Ultimately nothing

Theater an der Wien, where Fidelio *was first performed.*

existed for him as meaningfully as did music. The great middle years of Beethoven's career—the time that brought forth the symphonies heard here—were a period of breathtaking creativity. He was moving forward forcefully and without apology on all musical fronts—in the symphony, the concerto, the sonata, and chamber music. His one and only opera, *Fidelio*, finally reached a satisfactory form in 1814 after three painstaking revisions. Such relentless editing was typical of Beethoven. Though composing was cathartic for him, he suffered through extensive revision and rewriting. In this he could not have been more different from Mozart. Beethoven left behind sketchbooks containing various drafts and sketches that show the restless but sustained intensity of his effort.

In the last years of his life Beethoven became a towering figure of legend, a genius in a creative world of his own. His music became ever more formidable, so challenging, expansive, and sometimes harrowing that it still tests the patience of an unsuspecting audience. This Beethoven, the composer of the late string quartets and the final piano sonatas, can be difficult for listeners to embrace. Singers and choruses still shudder at the demands placed on them by his mighty *Missa Solemnis*. Some observers at the time flatly refused to consider his Ninth Symphony—a triumph at its premiere— a real symphony because of its vocal/choral finale.

Beethoven was both a Classical and a Romantic composer, proof, as one writer has said, that Romanticism was an idea that needed a Classical mind to conceive it. His training and influences were strictly Classical. The personal tragedy that befell him became a terrible victory, and it freed him to pursue his ideas about music without caring whether the aristocratic circles of Vienna approved. He prepared music for the great changes that would come in the Romantic age, and every composer who followed would work in his shadow.

Beethoven died on March 26, 1827. He was only fifty-six. He was already in poor health; his fatal illness was brought on by a fever that turned into pleurisy with complications. In so many ways a miserable and unhappy man, he was motivated and inspired to the end by pure ideals that seem at odds with his appalling personality: an unshakable belief in the dignity of man, so majestically captured in the Ninth Symphony, coupled with a profound love of nature. "How glad I shall be to wander among shrubs, forests, trees, herbs, and rocks!" he exulted in a letter to a friend. "No man can love the country as I do, for it is forests, trees, and rocks that provide men with the resonance they desire."

His Legacy

The breadth and depth of Beethoven's achievement have no equal, especially in their vigorous challenge to the listener's soul and mind. If his music was not always as pleasant and elegant as Mozart's, for instance, it was every bit as intense and meaningful. Virtually every musical form Beethoven encountered was changed by his effort, none more so than the symphony.

The late symphonies of Haydn and Mozart anticipated a weightier, more profound expression for the medium that was fulfilled by Beethoven without much explanation or warning. His first two symphonies were splendid pieces, nicely conceived and executed in the Classical mold. Then, however, his musical personality began to assert itself. The seven symphonies that followed were revelations, including the one Beethoven called "my little symphony," the Eighth, slipped in neatly between the Dionysian Seventh and the soaring Ninth.

Beethoven's symphonic testament was so influential that later composers would become superstitious about writing more than nine symphonies. The young Franz Schubert adored Beethoven and marched in the great man's funeral procession; he died a year later, leaving behind only nine completed symphonies. Beethoven's greatest and most direct heir, Johannes Brahms, was so intimidated by his example that he kept postponing the writing of a symphony. Brahms's first piano concerto was sketched originally as a

Bust of Beethoven

Franz Schubert (1797-1828)

symphony, but he changed his mind; his first symphony did not appear until after the composer was forty. (One misguided observer labeled it "Beethoven's Tenth," a nickname intended as a great compliment but one that Brahms found highly insulting.)

Brahms's contemporary Richard Wagner wrote only one symphony, a youthful failure, claiming later that Beethoven had said the last word about the symphony. Wagner believed the symphony should be abandoned in favor of his "music of the future," and that his massive music-dramas were the next logical step in the Beethoven tradition. As if to prove the point, Wagner conducted a performance of Beethoven's Ninth Symphony in 1872, when the cornerstone was laid for his festival opera house at Bayreuth, where Beethoven's tradition has echoed ever since.

Beethoven's symphonies have never left the repertoire of the world's orchestras. In fact, it might be said they formed the foundation of that repertoire, for in Beethoven's wake the performance of

Johannes Brahms (1833-1897)

Richard Wagner (1813-1883)

an established symphonic repertoire became a new musical standard. The nine symphonies were so widely performed during the nineteenth century that an enduring monograph about them by the British musical scholar Sir George Grove was published as early as 1896. They have been and remain the calling card of every notable conductor in the twentieth century, the ultimate test of a conductor's skill. The Beethoven bicentennial in 1970 threatened a marketing overkill with myriad recordings and performances—though nothing compared to the Mozart blowout twenty-one years later—but the public's taste for the symphonies barely abated.

A dramatic increase in the appreciation of the Beethoven symphonies came in the 1980s, when the original-instruments movement turned its attention from the Baroque and early Classical eras to the music of Beethoven's time. Using authentic instruments of the period, tuned to a lower pitch, and observing tempos that Beethoven might have chosen, these often controversial recordings and performances have reawakened the immediacy and stinging power of his music in a world made blasé by hundreds of recordings. The result is an ever-broadening understanding of Beethoven, whose symphonies we can now appreciate on several levels.

What Is a Symphony?

The word *symphony* has Greek roots. It means "a harmony of instrumental sounds" or "a sounding together," an apt description for the effect created by a modern work that bears this label. The way the word has been applied, however, has changed throughout the history of music.

In the seventeenth and early eighteenth centuries, a symphony (or *sinfonia*, in its Italian form) was usually a piece of music that the orchestra played before an opera, often in three contrasting sections, or movements, following a fast-slow-fast pattern. The term also described an orchestral interlude in an opera or an oratorio, such as the brief, gentle "Pastoral Symphony" in Handel's *Messiah*, which evokes the atmosphere present at the Nativity.

The symphony became the large-scale musical format we know today in the first half of the eighteenth century, as the Baroque era was giving way to the Classical. This shift reflected one especially important change, though there were many others, that was taking place in the texture of serious music. The change was a move away from polyphony—in which several musical lines or voices combine, with more or less equal weight, while retaining their identity—toward homophony, in which a single line or voice dominates, supported by a progression of chords or a more elaborate accompaniment. The result was a larger, richer musical canvas, and the symphony evolved quickly as the most eloquent way to exploit it.

The first symphonies were relatively short, usually in three movements, again in a fast-slow-fast pattern. Quite early in this process, the structure was expanded to include a fourth movement, a dance—usually a minuet—that appeared between the second and final movements. Most of the important early symphonists followed this structure. They were predominantly German and Austrian, though the Italian composer Giovanni Battista Sammartini (1700–1775) was also influential and wrote seventy-seven symphonies. Orchestral music had a special significance in the German city of Mannheim, where the symphony flourished in concerts for the court of the Elector of the Palatinate. With its splendid orchestra, lavishly supported by official policy, it was an important stop for all musicians in the mid-eighteenth century. (Mozart visited several times.) Mannheim's principal court composers, Johann Stamitz (1717–1757) and Ignaz Holzbauer (1711–1783), with their associates, developed the symphony there to a high degree of sophistication. Others were involved in similar work elsewhere, notably the Viennese composers Monn and Wagenseil and two of Johann Sebastian Bach's sons, Carl Philipp Emanuel and Johann Christian.

The turning point in the symphony's history came with the emergence of Franz Joseph Haydn (1732–1809), the prolific Austrian composer who is

Beethoven at the piano.

Franz Joseph Haydn (1732-1809)

misleadingly called the Father of the Symphony. If not the format's sire, Haydn was among its greatest innovators. His work suggested limitless possibilities for the symphony, and in his hands it became the ultimate musical medium. Haydn also developed the use of sonata form as a basic outline for the composition of a symphony. Though he was an impeccable Classical composer, Haydn's symphonies—there are 104 of them—are anything but predictable. They vary, from work to work, in the number of movements they employ, in the order of those movements, and, most vividly, in the character of their music. Haydn used everything in his symphonies—folk songs and tunes from his own operas, barnyard noises, and everyday sounds—and gave them curious but appropriate titles such as *Hornsignal, The Bear, The Hen,* and *Drumroll.*

Haydn was already an eminent figure in music when Wolfgang Amadeus Mozart (1756–1791) emerged on the scene, and each was the other's biggest fan. In his own eloquent way, Mozart carried forward Haydn's freewheeling, sophisticated ideas, and rose to as yet unattained heights of expression in the final three of his forty-one numbered symphonies. Haydn, who outlived Mozart by eighteen years, frequently remarked on how much he learned from his young friend. Haydn's greatest symphonies, the final twelve written for concerts in London, were magnificent works that summed up, in his beautifully articulate manner, his experience with the symphonic form. This was the state of the symphony when the young Beethoven arrived in Vienna.

Beethoven had no intention of claiming either Mozart or Haydn as his model. Like both of them, however, he was a master of sonata form, and he had imaginative ideas about what the symphony could be. His third symphony, titled *Eroica*, was a stunning challenge to prevailing ideas about what the medium could express, and how. The *Pastoral* used five movements, each of which had a title. Most audaciously, the Ninth Symphony ended with a massive choral finale that was as long as some Classical symphonies in their entirety.

The effect of Beethoven's nine symphonies on the course of music is incalculable. Some contemporaries were appalled by their intensity. After hearing the Fifth Symphony, the German poet and philosopher Johann Wolfgang von Goethe, not quite meaning to flatter, said, "How big it is—quite wild!

Wolfgang Amadeus Mozart (1756-1791)

Enough to bring the house about one's ears!" Even if stunned, most sophisticated listeners knew they had heard something visionary. The French composer Hector Berlioz, whose life was changed by his encounter with these works, recalled in his *Memoirs* the response of his teacher Le Sueur to the confounding bombardment of the Fifth Symphony: "Out! Let me get out; I must have air. . . . It's incredible! Marvelous! It has so upset and bewildered me that when I wanted to put on my hat, *I couldn't find my head* . . . . One ought not to write music like that!"

Sonata Form

Sonata form is a musical structure that offers a floor plan for the opening movement of a sonata, a string quartet, a concerto, or a symphony. It also suggests the relationship of musical keys to be used within the movement.

To appreciate and enjoy Beethoven's symphonies, it is not necessary to know and understand sonata form. As the craft that supports the art, sonata form is most effective when the listener is not even aware of it. Where Beethoven is concerned, the inspiration and quality of his work are so extraordinary that we do not have to think about how he gets from A to Z—we want to follow him anyway. What sonata form offers the composer is a method for organizing his musical ideas and creating a tension that can be resolved in an interesting and compelling manner.

While the rules of sonata form frequently change, especially in Romantic music, the standard design generally holds in Classical works.

In the opening section, called the exposition, two themes are presented, usually contrasting both in character and in their keys. The first theme is sometimes repeated before a modulation leads into the second major section, called the development. Here, material from the exposition is elaborated upon—sometimes at length and with great complexity—as it works its way back into the original key. Once that is achieved, the first theme is repeated, signaling the beginning of the recapitulation, where the music of the exposition is heard again but in an altered form. It is often followed by the coda, a section that contains the cadenza and carries the entire movement to its conclusion.

What about the symphony's remaining movements? There are usually  three, though Beethoven's Sixth Symphony has four. Beethoven eliminated the minuet as a third movement, developing in its place the *scherzo*. The Italian word *scherzo* means "joke," and that sets the tone for this particular movement, which, though not always light-hearted or friendly, is brisk and in striking contrast to the slow movement that usually precedes it. The second, slow movement provides a contrasting period of calm after the domineering action of the first movement.

Vienna today.

Within these movements, structure can vary. Beethoven was fond, for instance, of taking a theme and creating a series of variations upon it. The slow movements of both symphonies heard here have a theme-and-variations unity. In all of Beethoven's symphonies, the final movements are monumental utterances that represent a great summing-up, whether it is a shout of triumph, as in the Fifth Symphony, or a grateful benediction, as in the Sixth.

The Recordings

SYMPHONY NO. 5 IN C MINOR, *Op. 67*

Beethoven probably began toying with ideas for the Fifth Symphony sometime in 1804, but did not begin serious work on it until 1807. He completed it the following year, while he was also at work on the *Pastoral*. Fierce and explosive, the Fifth Symphony is Beethoven's first in a minor key and is shaped by an initial crisis, increasing conflict, and, finally, hard-won harmony. It is a lean and concise work of astonishing originality that adheres to the traditional shape of the Classical symphony while making it a very different vehicle for expression.

Despite the many labels that have been slapped on it, this symphony does not seem specifically to be *about* anything. Like the *Pastoral,* it is dedicated to Prince von Lobkowitz and Count Rasumovsky, noble patrons of the composer who shared his progressive views. The vigor and energy with which Beethoven resolves its musical conflict probably parallel the nature and determination of his egalitarian political beliefs, though there is no evidence that he intended it to express any political message. Nor is there any real evidence, other than the statement of Anton Schindler, his notoriously unreliable secretary and biographer, that the symphony's famous first four notes represent "Fate knocking at the door." The famous scholar and musicologist Heinrich Schencker scuttled this myth by noting that he had found the same motive in Beethoven's G major piano concerto. "Was this another door on which Fate knocked or was someone else knocking on the same door?" he asked.

THE FIRST MOVEMENT *Allegro con brio (Quickly, with spirit).* Beethoven's musical signature is the shocking thunder-clap in four notes with which this symphony begins. The first fifty-eight measures of the first movement are built on nothing more than this musical phrase, variously repeated, with the same hammering, rhythmic pattern and the same interval in pitch between the first three notes and the fourth. Suddenly (1 0:56), a horn call in a new key heralds the arrival of relief:

Oboe solo from Allegro con brio.

33

a second melodic subject, a singing melody of such imploring sweetness that it seems to calm the fury that has been raging. The four-note phrase remains in the background, nervously pulsing in the new key, now chastened by its encounter with the second subject. This section, called the exposition because it announces the movement's principal themes, is then repeated in its entirety. In the development section (1 1:57), the principal themes are explored and worked out in new ways. The violent thrust of the opening measures returns, piling on the four-note phrase relentlessly, occasionally in different guises. The tension increases, stammering with a frenzy verging on incoherence, until the movement's opening bars return (1 3:36), now voiced differently in the orchestra. Then, the briefest moment of poetic repose—a free-form solo for the oboe (1 5:43)—breaks the tension and brings on the end of the development. Another flourish of C major introduces the coda (1 6:23), the concluding section of the movement that, in this case, sums up the "action." The only new material in the coda is a melodic subject (1 7:56) that re-emphasizes the catharsis with which the entire movement concludes.

THE SECOND MOVEMENT *Andante con moto (Moving along, with motion).* An entirely different mood emerges in the second movement. Beethoven spins a series of variations on a lovely, long-breathed theme that appears and quickly unfolds. A variation emerges in the woodwinds (2 0:26), sweetly echoing elements in the principal theme, and leads directly to the second theme (2 1:01), a march of nobly rising phrases that creates a powerful sense of anticipation. (In a variation, the basic melody is embellished and elaborated on, sometimes slightly, sometimes in a way that alters the melody to the point of reinventing it. The variations with which Beethoven built this andante never cease to amaze in their lucid and tightly focused invention, expressive range, and unsurpassed beauty.) Listen carefully to the principal themes—their rhythms, the harmonies that support them, and their melodic profiles—and the variations that follow will seem even more ingenious. This musical adventure reaches its conclusion in an atmosphere of great tenderness and beauty (②9:41), until one is jerked back to reality (②10:35) by a final, monumental surge from the orchestra that recalls the first movement.

THE THIRD MOVEMENT *Allegro (Quickly)*. This is the symphony's scherzo, though it is not labeled that way. This brief movement observes the plan of the scherzo, with the usual repeats and a contrasting trio section to lighten the mood. The abrupt ending of the andante is revisited: As in the opening of the first movement, the key is C minor and the mood is tense. It opens quietly, in a melody played with an eerily light touch by the cellos and basses and echoed uneasily in the violins. This dialogue is repeated and extended slightly, then extinguished by a swaggering, almost macho melody (③0:19) in the horns (a rhythmic echo of that key four-note phrase that opens the first movement), bolstered by brusque chords from the strings. Both themes are explored and developed until the orchestra comes to rest, suddenly and disarmingly, on a C—the jumping-off point for the trio section (③1:53), which begins with a whimsical melody that erupts from the cellos and basses and spreads. After a repeat, the second section of the trio (③2:30) seems to be a comical twist on the first, with hesitations and lurches that lead to an elaboration of the theme. The whole musical mood moderates and softens, with the flute bringing it back to earth in a gentle landing. The mysterious atmosphere of the movement's opening gathers once more (③3:30), but with striking changes. When the first two melodies are heard again, there are rich nuances in the quiet combination of instruments, dominated by the strings playing pizzicato. The mood shifts suddenly ([3] 4:42), with a soft, magically insistent and irregular pulse from the timpani and an allusion to the opening melody that hesitates before rising to a tremulous crescendo. It leads, without a pause, into the Fourth Movement.

THE FOURTH MOVEMENT *Allegro* (*Quickly*). Here is the moment we have been waiting for: resolution, the light at the end of the tunnel, victory, *home*. The crescendo that leads out of the scherzo explodes into a thrilling, exultant melody that arrives like a victory march, sounded by everything Beethoven can muster: trombones (for the first time in this piece), double bassoon, and piccolo, with the timpani pounding away underneath it all. It is quickly contrasted by a striking and noble passage sung by the winds ([4] 0:39) and dominated by the horns. It leads into a third passage ([4] 1:09) that is, once again, dominated by three short notes followed by a fourth longer one; this phrase, repeated and turned upside down, is an important element in the development of the final movement. As it is developed, it connects with the second major theme of this movement ([4] 1:39), introduced in the clarinet and violas and explored variously, until the entire first section is repeated. The development section follows and plays with the four-note phrase introduced earlier, a game that grows increasingly frenzied and thunderous until it suddenly gives way to a teasing echo of the scherzo ([4] 6:14), followed by a bewitching passage for the oboe that leads to the recapitulation of the movement's opening ([4] 6:50). The magnificent coda then begins ([4] 7:30). The themes heard here, familiar from earlier in the movement, are now transformed, jubilantly tossed about, and further ennobled as the end draws near. The effect is astonishing—the music seems to beat like a heart, faster and faster, as its goal looms in sight (☐4 8:32). As it hurries along, the music so surely and emphatically celebrates its achievement that the incessant pounding of the C-major chords adds a smile to the sense of relief and gratitude that brings this stormy work to a close.

SYMPHONY NO. 6 IN F MAJOR, *Op. 68, ("Pastoral")*

The Symphony No. 6 in F, known as the *Pastoral,* turns every expectation created by the Fifth on its head. The *Pastoral,* a personal meditation on the glories of nature, is elaborately labeled, movement by movement, in a manner unique to the time. Despite his descriptions, Beethoven was more interested in the spirit created by these images than in literal detail. He may have had second thoughts about giving the audience the impression that he was merely picturing nature and, in the published score, added to the title the words, *"Mehr Ausdruck der Empfindung als Mahlerei"* ("More an expression of feeling than a painting").

Beethoven profoundly loved the outdoors and, when he could, spent hours on long walks. Witnesses have described the spectacle of Beethoven hurtling through the Viennese woods at a furious pace, shouting, singing, conducting an imaginary orchestra, pausing only to jot down ideas in his sketchbook. The images he conjured in the *Pastoral* probably came from the area around Heiligenstadt, near Vienna. The impact the *Pastoral* had on Romantic music is immense. The purity of its expression gives us a glimpse of the passionate soul and great heart behind Beethoven's formidable personality. "Almighty in the forest!" he wrote once. "I am happy, blissful in the forest: every tree speaks. O God, what splendor! In such a wooded scene, in the heights, there is calm, calm in which to serve Him."

THE FIRST MOVEMENT *Erwachen heiterer Empfindungen bei der Ankunft auf dem Lande (Awakening of Cheerful Feelings Upon Arrival in the Country).* There is no mistaking the inspiration of this symphony: You hear it immediately, in a melody as pure and jauntily invigorating as nature itself, sung by the violins over held (or pedal) tones in the violas and cellos. If ever a symphonic movement could be said to blossom, this one does. The principal melody gives birth, by quotation or variation, to every other bud of a melody heard here. "It would be difficult to find in Art a greater amount of confidence, not to say audacity, than Beethoven has furnished by his incessant repetition of the same or similar short phrases throughout this long movement," Sir

George Grove wrote, "and yet the effect is such that when the end arrives, we would gladly hear it all over again." The way Beethoven develops and explores this melody reflects the organic inevitability of nature itself. The music moves like an eager gaze traveling across the rural panorama, taking it all in, until a second melody appears in the cello (⑤ 1:22), as if to suggest— quite clearly, at one point (⑤ 1:52)—a gathering breeze. The development begins (⑤ 2:45) by repeating variously the opening notes of the principal theme. It gives way (⑤ 3:00) to another fragment of that theme, which is variously repeated, handed off, and transformed as it strides across ninety-two measures, pausing every now and then before progressing further. The recapitulation (⑤ 6:07) is no mere restatement of the movement's opening section: Beethoven transforms the material by having the orchestra sing the theme in different voices. The pleasure captured by the music seems to grow more urgent in the brief coda (⑤ 8:15), as if to indicate a quiet ecstasy. It is pierced only by piquant sounds in the woodwinds (⑤ 9:22) that suggest bird-song, a droll touch that brings the first movement to a simple, sublime close.

THE SECOND MOVEMENT *Szene am Bach (Scene by the Brook).*
From the first bar, Beethoven evokes a gently murmuring brook in the second violins, the violas, and the cellos; the sound carries on its surface a tender melody in the violins. As is usual with Beethoven, the tunes are breathtakingly simple; it is what he does with them that boggles the mind. In the opening seconds of this andante, for instance, the violins' melody is passed off to the clarinet (⑥ 0:36), as the rest of the orchestra subtly weaves a new atmospheric texture. A melodic rise and fall (⑥ 1:02) follow the same course, and, after

The banks of the Danube, east of Vienna.

an interlude, the melody returns (⑥1:44), transformed and led in a new direction by a phrase (⑥2:12) Sir George Grove calls "the murmur of a happy Pan." As the music flows along, the bassoon announces the limpid tune that will be the movement's second principal theme (⑥2:43). The treatment of this material is enchanting, moving from voice to voice effortlessly and with ever-imaginative handling. The development section (⑥4:07) begins with a striking change in the opening violin theme, now with the woodwinds offering the accompaniment. What follows is a shimmering fantasy on these themes, a sound-picture so rich, so subtly evocative that it speaks best for itself. With the murmur of the brook never far away, the themes mingle and transform themselves like the fleeting sensations of a beautiful spring afternoon. The brief but unforgettable coda (⑥10:05) is a ravishing benediction (⑥10:42) of birdsong from the nightingale (the flute), the quail (the oboe), and the cuckoo (clarinet).

THE THIRD MOVEMENT *Lustiges Zusammensein der Landleute* (*Merry Gathering of the Country Folk*). People finally appear on Beethoven's canvas in this scherzo movement, enjoying a rustic dance party. The composer captures the spirit of a country dance and its lack of pretension. The vigor of the party is suggested immediately by the pointed energy of the opening theme, followed by a phrase for strings and flute that recalls the sound of a rustic instrument like a bagpipe. A high-stepping dance is well under way (⑦0:30), with raucous retorts from the horns. With support from the bassoon, the oboe sings a new melody (⑦0:53), which is picked up by the clarinet and then the horn, creating a kind of chatter. A brusque new dance sensation appears (⑦1:35), carrying on with great abandon and ending as suddenly as it began. All of this is repeated (⑦2:20) with new energy and intensity until the last seconds of the movement (⑦5:16), when the mood suddenly darkens and the party breaks up and flees in panic.

THE FOURTH MOVEMENT *Gewitter, Sturm* (*Thunder, Storm*).
This is the shortest symphonic movement Beethoven ever wrote, and here less is definitely more. The sound and fury of a thunderstorm are captured with stunning immediacy. The lashing of rain and wind, bolts of lightning, and claps of thunder are easy to isolate. Listen, though, to the fraught atmosphere of the moments of calm (⑧1:20) and the faint rumbling of thunder in the strings that announces another frightening wave of wind and rain. The music continues without relief until it spends itself and fades away (⑧2:58), leaving behind an uneasy quiet.

The Storm from Gewitter, Sturm.

THE FIFTH MOVEMENT *Hirtengesang: Frohe and dankbare Gefühle nach dem Sturm* (*Shepherd's Song: Happy and Thankful Feelings After the Storm*).
The calm following the storm has arrived. The oboe hints at this relief, and the clarinet (⑨0:19) suggests the song of the cuckoo. That song is taken up

by the horn, where it suggests yodeling, and then is handed off to the violins. It is transformed (⑨0:36) into a humble but radiant hymn of thanksgiving sung by shepherds who have weathered another storm in the meadow. The succeeding sections of the hymn add to the sense of joy and gratitude, with contrast arriving (⑨2:57) in a soothing new melody—the movement's second principal theme—in the clarinets and bassoons. The remainder of the movement repeats and embellishes the two principal themes, suggesting the kaleidoscopic sensations of relief and joy after a trial. They mingle and build to a final burst of ecstatic gratitude (⑨7:22), and recede into what seems to be an intensely personal moment of reverie for the happy mortal, once again content and renewed in the rugged majesty of nature.

The Performers

The German-born conductor and composer André Previn (1929–) grew up in the United States, a refugee from the Nazi regime, after early study at the Berlin Hochschule für Musik and the Paris Conservatoire. He continued his studies in Los Angeles, where his father's cousin scored music for films. While still a teenager, Previn began orchestrating and composing film scores at MGM. A lucrative and successful film career followed, during which he won Academy Awards for scoring *An American in Paris, Gigi, Porgy and Bess,* and *My Fair Lady.* His diverse musical interests—he had also developed into a fine jazz pianist—led him to study conducting with Pierre Monteux while

André Previn

stationed in San Francisco during a tour of duty in the U.S. Army. In 1962 he made his conducting debut in St. Louis, and shortly thereafter he left film to build an outstanding reputation as a conductor and as a serious composer. In addition to a prodigious multimedia career, Previn has been principal conductor of the Houston Symphony Orchestra (1967–1969), the London Symphony Orchestra (1968–1979, also conductor emeritus), the Pittsburgh Symphony Orchestra (1976–1984), the Royal Philharmonic Orchestra (1985–1987), and the Los Angeles Philharmonic Orchestra (1985–1990).

Rudolf Kempe

The German conductor Rudolf Kempe (1910–1976) had a distinctive personal style, a quick intelligence, and a thoughtful musicality that made him a favorite of both musicians and conductors. Trained in the orchestra school of the Dresden Staatskapelle, he was playing principal oboe in the Gewandhaus Orchestra of Leipzig when he made his conducting debut, saving a performance by stepping in at the last moment. This feat led to an offer to conduct and laid the ground for a new career. After holding posts in Weimar and Chemnitz, Kempe returned to his native Dresden in 1949 to head the Dresden Staatsoper. Four years later he began a celebrated tenure as musical director of the Munich Opera. His later decision to relinquish such operatic posts led to a new phase in his career, as a critically acclaimed and beloved guest conductor, both in concert and in recordings. He continued to conduct opera occasionally in Munich and London, as he had so brilliantly at the Salzburg and Bayreuth festivals. Just before his death in 1976, Kempe had accepted an appointment as principal conductor of the BBC Symphony Orchestra.

CREDITS:

Austrian Cultural Institute, New York: 13, 15, 18, 31, 38; Erich Lessing/Art Resource, New York: 16; The Bettmann Archive: 10, 24, 27, 28; EMI Records, Ltd./photo by Walter H. Scott: 43; EMI Records, Ltd./photo by Mirschel: 44; EMI Records, Ltd.: Cover, 20, 29; Dover Publications, Inc.: 22, 23; The British Museum: 14.

With special thanks to the Austrian Cultural Institute, New York.